DREAMLAND

Introduction to CODING

CONCEPT BY
ANUJ CHAWLA

EDITED BY
LATA SETH

DREAMLAND PUBLICATIONS
J-128, KIRTI NAGAR, NEW DELHI-110 015, INDIA
PHONE : +91-11-2510 6050, 2543 5657
E-mail : dreamland@dreamlandpublications.com
Shop online at www.dreamlandpublications.com
Follow us on www.instagram.com/dreamland.publications

Published in 2022 by

DREAMLAND PUBLICATIONS

J-128, Kirti Nagar, New Delhi - 110 015, India

Tel : +91-11-2510 6050, 2543 5657

E-mail : dreamland@dreamlandpublications.com

www.dreamlandpublications.com

ABOUT THIS BOOK

Kids love mysteries and secret messages written in code. This book offers plenty of fun spy puzzles, mazes, secret codes that will keep the children challenged and entertained from start to finish. Using codes of various sorts, crosswords, word searches, and other cleverly designed activities, they will learn some amazing lessons and facts about the world as they enjoy decoding the codes.

Suitable for ages 6 plus, this book is perfect for the age-group's coding-decoding skills with games and mystery messages to solve. Children can crack codes and make up their own codes to use with their friends to send secret messages.

So, let's get set and solve alphabet and number codes, picture puzzles and more!

LET'S UNDERSTAND CODING-DECODING

Coding is an art. When we think of coding, we think of computers, but codes are all around us. Codes and methods of secret communication are in use since ancient time. Throughout history, humans have created many different codes for communicating.

Some codes are used to send secret messages, while others deliver information across long distances. Coding is a method of transmitting a message between the sender and the receiver that no third person can understand it.

The person, who transmits the code or signal, is called the sender and the person who receives it, is called the receiver. Transmitted codes or signals are decoded on the other side by the receiver - this is known as decoding.

There are different types of coding and decoding tests.

Letter Coding — Alphabets in a word are replaced by other alphabets according to a specific rule to know its code.

Number Coding — In this, each alphabet or words are assigned to the numeric values. To solve this we should observe the given letters and the assigned values and use the same rule to find the value of the given code.

Substitution — In this section, object names are substituted with different object names. We should carefully trace the substitution and answer the given question.

The coding and decoding tests are set up to judge the candidate's ability to decipher the rule that has been followed to code a particular word/message and break the code to decipher the message.

DECODE ME

Follow the directions to discover message!

| C | | | | | |

| Forward 3 | Down 1 Back 1 | Down 3 | Forward 4 Up 2 | Up 1 Forward 1 | Down 2 Back 1 |

| | | | | | |

| Down 2 Back 2 | Down 1 Back 1 | | Down 1 Forward 2 | Forward 1 Up 2 | Forward 1 Up 1 |

START	A	Q	C	P	U	R	M
	I	U	O	I	D	O	E	N
	H	C	B	B	K	T	I	S
	J	D	A	N	H	E	G	O
	I	N	D	G	L	S	T	N
	V	M	F	Z	I	R	U	X
	W	F	L	S	Y	Q	V	P
	I	D	K	E	X	F	W	G

SECRET MESSAGE

Use the code to help figure out the secret message.

A	=	26
B	=	25
C	=	24
D	=	23
E	=	22
F	=	21
G	=	20
H	=	19
I	=	18
J	=	17
K	=	16
L	=	15
M	=	14
N	=	13
O	=	12
P	=	11
Q	=	10
R	=	9
S	=	8
T	=	7
U	=	6
V	=	5
W	=	4
X	=	3
Y	=	2
Z	=	1

___ ___ ___ ___ ___　　　　___ ___ ___ ___
13   22   5   22   9　　　　　 11   15   26   2

___ ___ ___ ___　　___ ___ ___　___ ___ ___ ___
4   18   7   19　　 14   26   7　 24   19   22   8

If you see another child
playing with matches or
a lighter, tell an adult
immediately.

BINARY

Follow the directions to find the code!

Use the binary code to write your name.

1 = Red   O = Green

Example : Lois

A	01000001	G	01000111	M	01001101	S	01010011	y	01011001
B	01000010	H	01001000	N	01001110	T	01010100	Z	01011010
C	01000011	I	01001001	O	01001111	U	10101010		
D	01000100	J	01001010	P	01010000	V	10010110		
E	01000101	K	01000001	Q	01010001	W	01010111		
F	01000110	L	01001100	R	01010010	X	01011000		

BINARY

Follow the directions to find the code!

Use the binary code to write the initials of your name.
1 = Red   O = Green
Example : LC

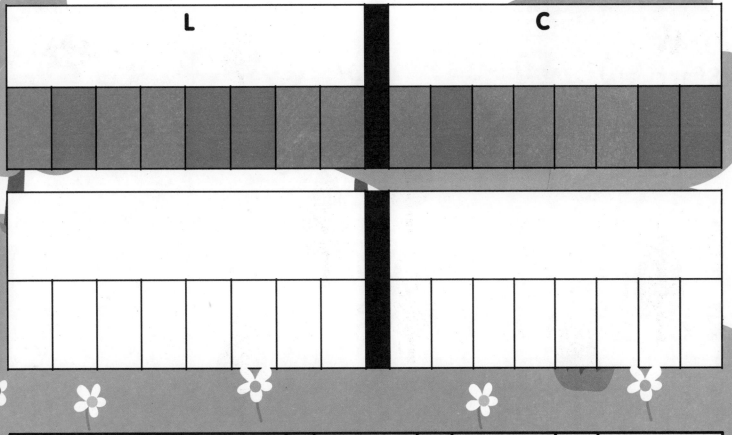

A	01000001	G	01000111	M	01001101	S	01010011	Y	01011001
B	01000010	H	01001000	N	01001110	T	01010100	Z	01011010
C	01000011	I	01001001	O	01001111	U	10101010		
D	01000100	J	01001010	P	01010000	V	10010110		
E	01000101	K	01000001	Q	01010001	W	01010111		
F	01000110	L	01001100	R	01010010	X	01011000		

Let's Explore

Jessica needs to find her way home through the enchanted forest. Below is the forest map. Follow the directions to step from dot to dot until you reach home! Draw a path through the dots as you find your way.

DIRECTIONS

Go 2 Dots East, 3 Dots South, 1 Dot East, 2 Dots South, 3 Dots West, 1 Dot South, 4 Dots East, 3 Dots North, 1 Dot East, 2 Dots North, 3 Dots East, 5 Dots South, 1 Dot West, 1 Dot South

North
West   East
South

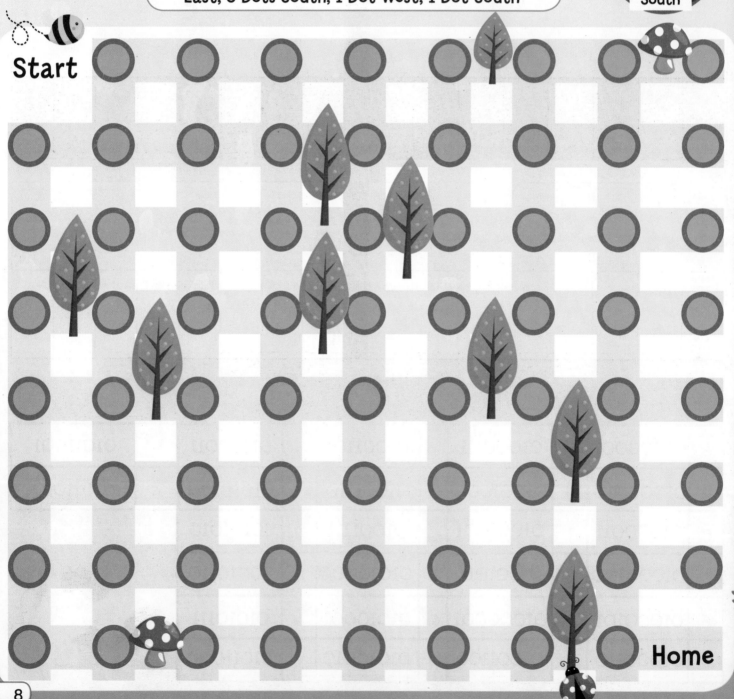

Start

Home

Let's Explore

James needs to find her way home through the jungle. Below is the forest map. Follow the directions to step from dot to dot until you reach home! Draw a path through the dots as you find your way.

DIRECTIONS

Go 4 dots Right, 4 dots Down, 1 dots Left, 2 Dots Down, 2 Dots Right, 4 Dots Up, 1 Dot Right, 1 Dot Down, 1 Dot right, 4 Dots Down

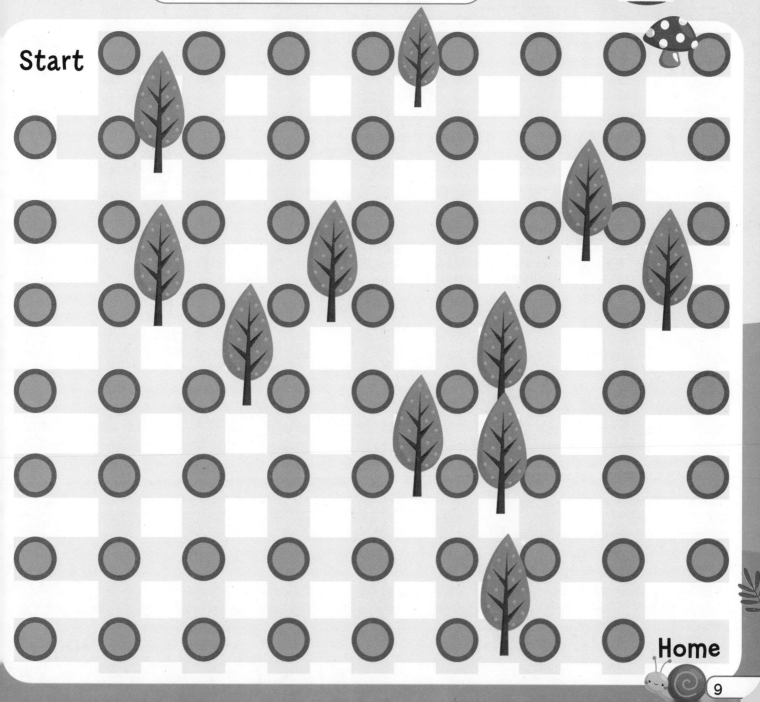

Start

Home

Let's Explore

Now it's your turn. Create your own map and write down the directions to find your way home.

DIRECTIONS

Up

Left ✦ Right

Down

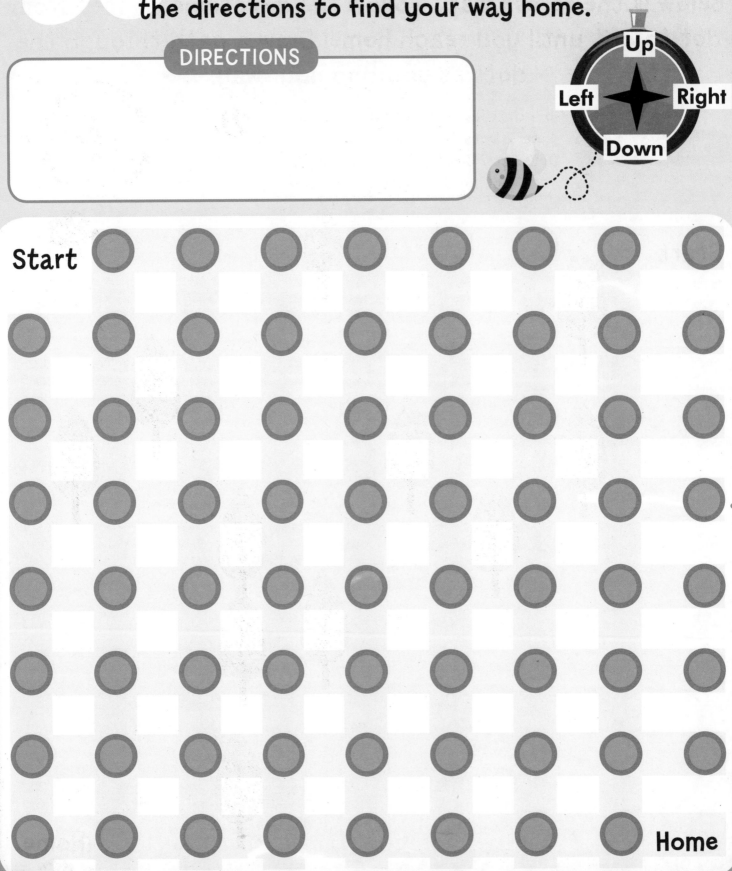

Start

Home

Let's Explore

Now it's your turn. Create your own map and write down the directions to find your way home.

DIRECTIONS

North

West   East

South

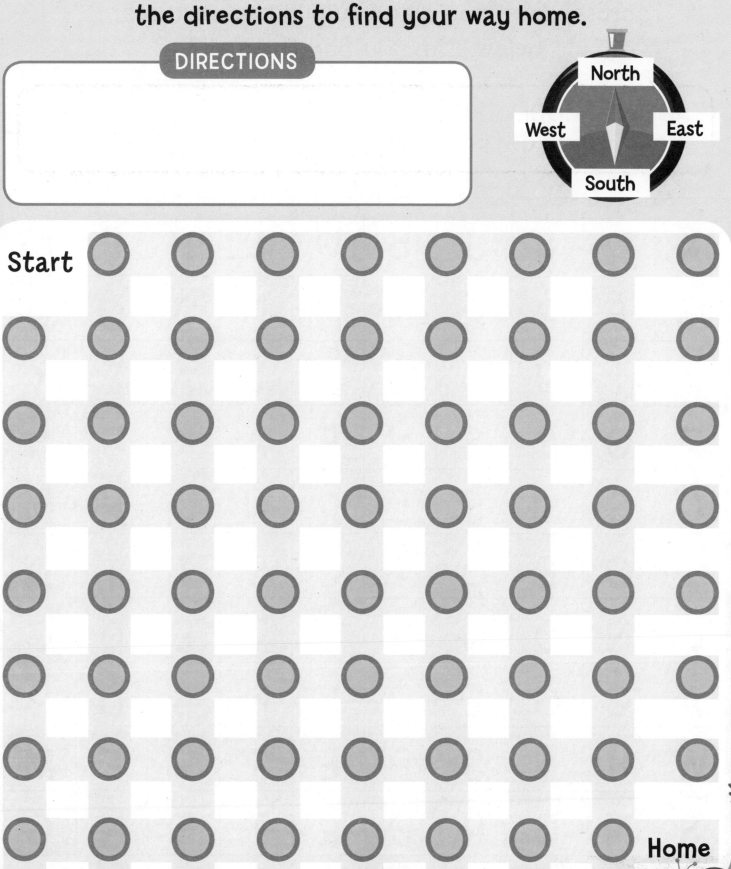

Start

Home

11

Word Search

The secret's out! These spy words are hidden across, down and diagonally in the word search below. Can you find them all?

AGENT   CODE   HIDDEN   MISSION   PLANS   SECRET
SNEAKY   SPY   UNDERCOVER   WHISPER

X	U	S	J	B	U	L	P	P	N
M	F	P	A	N	N	P	J	O	C
A	I	Y	O	G	D	L	A	E	K
Z	Q	S	S	N	E	A	K	Y	H
C	S	M	S	L	R	N	U	H	M
I	O	E	U	I	C	S	T	I	D
U	N	D	C	R	O	V	E	D	G
A	C	G	E	R	V	N	S	D	P
W	H	I	S	P	E	R	Y	E	M
S	N	C	R	D	R	T	E	N	G

Let's Explore

Find the words below amongst the jumble of letters.

MOUSE   INPUT   DATA   VIDEO   WEB
CODING   PATTERN   OUTPUT   ROBOT   PIXEL

P	I	X	E	L	A	Z	V
C	N	R	O	B	O	T	V
O	P	D	W	W	E	B	I
D	U	A	O	M	I	P	D
I	T	T	M	O	U	S	E
N	V	A	B	U	O	X	O
G	O	U	T	P	U	T	L
Z	P	A	T	T	E	R	N

Word Search

Find the words below amongst the jumble of letters.

CODING ROBOTICS DIGITAL MOBILE PIXEL
DATA VIDEO THINKING TECHNOLOGY
ROBOT PATTERN MOUSE INPUT OUTPUT WEB

C	Y	G	O	L	O	N	H	C	E	T	T	O	O
M	O	U	S	E	E	G	G	V	W	A	S	U	Y
X	W	D	D	Q	P	I	N	L	E	V	T	E	V
H	P	P	I	X	E	L	I	C	B	P	Z	X	N
V	G	I	G	N	F	S	K	D	U	M	A	T	R
I	V	N	I	P	G	D	N	T	Y	O	O	L	E
D	Q	P	T	P	C	A	I	D	P	B	N	M	T
E	O	U	A	F	J	T	H	K	O	I	U	Z	T
O	X	T	L	E	W	A	T	R	N	L	P	N	A
P	R	O	B	O	T	I	C	S	F	E	P	C	P

Decoding Sight Words

Use the number and letter grid to decode these common sight words.

Example

h	i	s
6	7	10

1	2	3	4	5	6	7	8	9	10	11	12
a	b	d	e	f	h	i	n	o	s	t	w

___

1 8 3   2 4   7 8

___

7 11   9 5   11 6 1 11

___

11 6 4   11 9   6 9 12

Decoding Sight Words

Use the number and letter grid to uncover common sight words.

Example

t	h	e
11	4	2

1	2	3	4	5	6	7	8	9	10	11	12	13	14	15
a	e	f	h	i	m	n	o	r	s	t	u	v	w	y

_____ _____ _____
4   1   10   3   8   9   1   9   2

_____ _____ _____
14   5   11   4   1   11   14   4   8   6

_____ _____ _____
5   10   8   7   3   9   8   6

Decoding Technology Words

Use the number and letter grid to decode these common technology words.

d	a	t	a
4	1	20	1

1	2	3	4	5	6	7	8	9	10	11	12	13
a	b	c	d	e	f	g	h	i	j	k	l	m

14	15	16	17	18	19	20	21	22	23	24	25	26
n	o	p	q	r	s	t	u	v	w	x	y	z

_____

3 15 4 9 14 7   13 5 13 15 18 25

_____

19 3 18 5 5 14   4 9 19 11

_____

3 15 16 25   3 21 20

_____

19 1 22 5   13 15 21 19 5

_____

16 1 19 20 5   16 18 9 14 20

Decoding Technology Words

Use the number and letter grid to decode these common technology words.

1	2	3	4	5	6	7	8	9	10	11	12	13
a	b	c	d	e	f	g	h	i	j	k	l	m

14	15	16	17	18	19	20	21	22	23	24	25	26
n	o	p	q	r	s	t	u	v	w	x	y	z

_____

5 13 1 9 12   9 14 20 5 18 14 5 20

_____

22 9 18 21 19   11 5 25 2 15 1 18 4

_____

2 9 14 1 18 25   2 25 20 5

_____

3 1 2 12 5   4 15 23 14 12 15 1 4

_____

9 3 15 14   16 9 24 5 12

Decode the Word

Fill in the letters from the clues provided and draw the pictures for each word.

3	21	16

19	20	5	23	16	1	14

22	21	12	20	21	18	5

11	14	9	6	5

15	3	20	15	16	21	19

10	5	12	12	25	6	9	19	8

a	b	c	d	e	f	g	h	i	j	k	l	m	n	o	p	q	r	s	t	u	v	w	x	y	z
1	2	3	4	5	6	7	8	9	10	11	12	13	14	15	16	17	18	19	20	21	22	23	24	25	26

Decoding Days

Use the code box to write the letters above the numbered spaces below.

Example

H E L L O

A D E F H I L M

N O R S T U W Y

1
2
3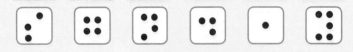
4
5
6
7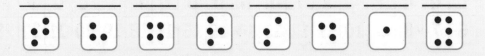

Batman

Batman is the name of an actual city in which country?
Write the name of each picture in its space. One letter
from each word will spell out the answer.

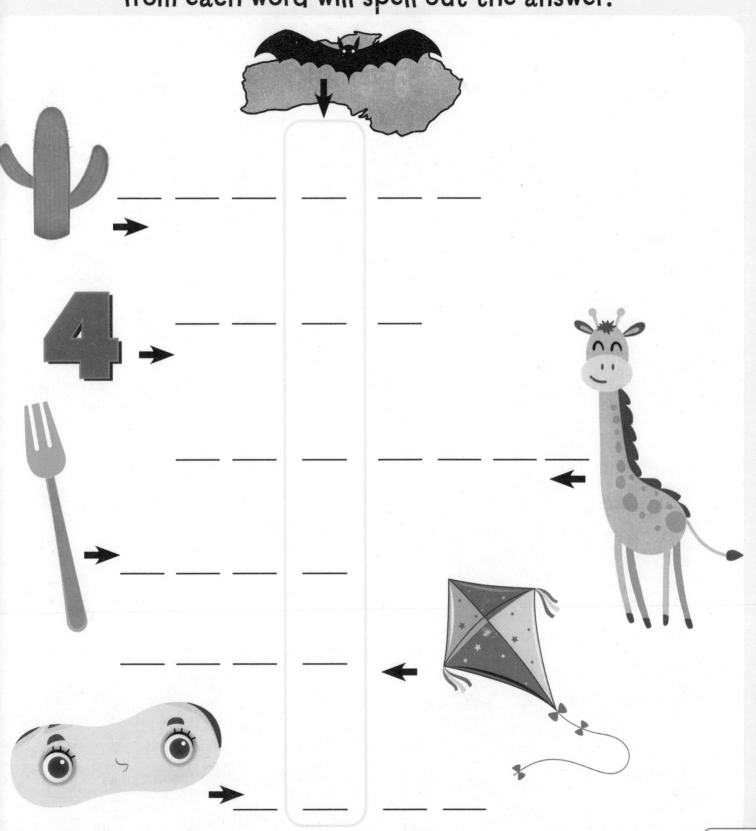

Symbol Letter Code

Use the code key below to decode the sentence. Have fun!

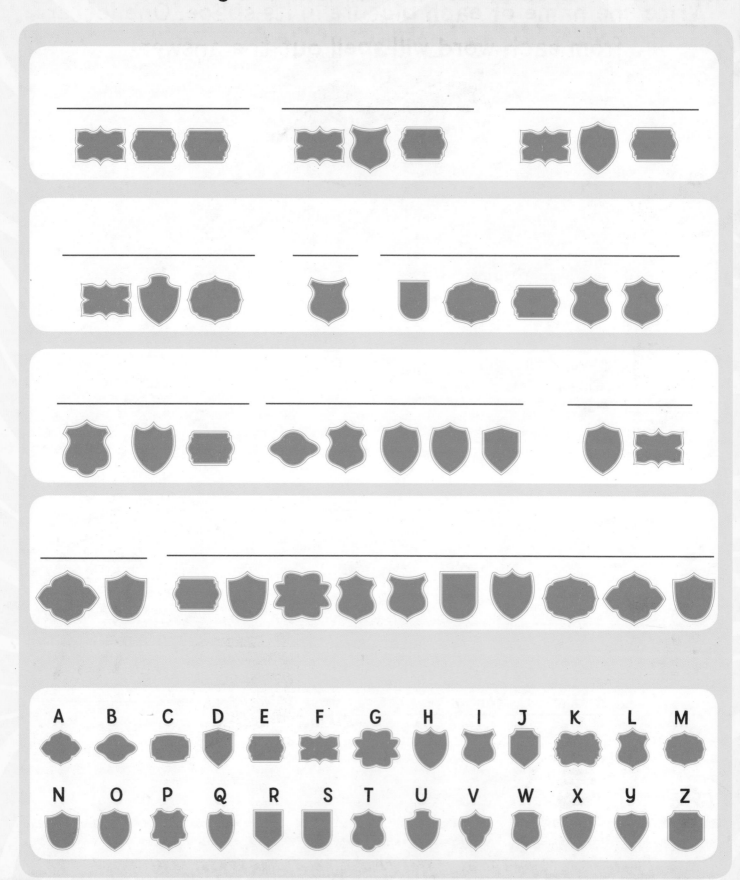

Decode Message

Break the code by writing an alphabet for each picture.

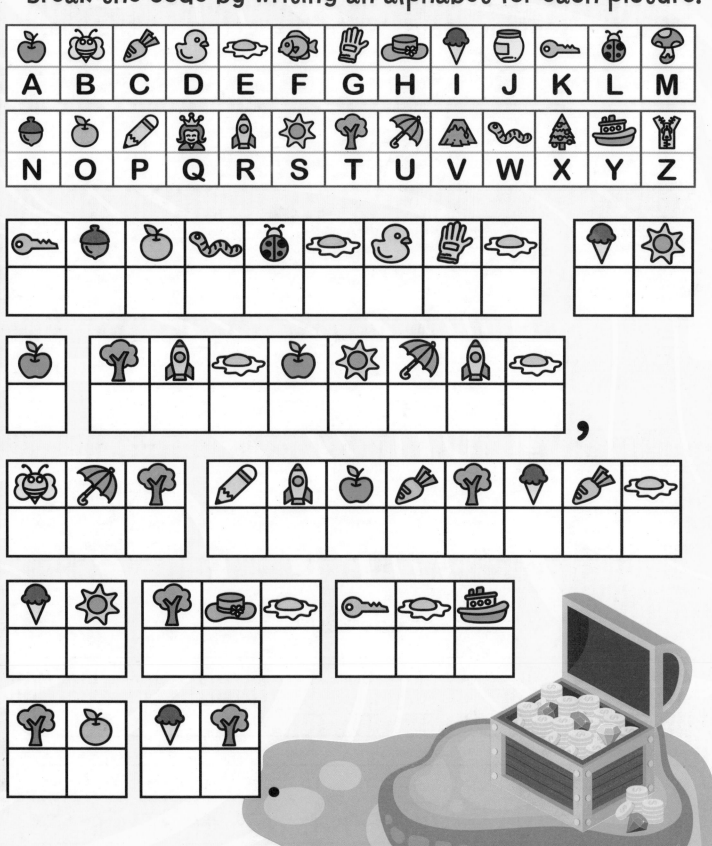

| | | | | | | | | | | | | | |
|A|B|C|D|E|F|G|H|I|J|K|L|M|

| | | | | | | | | | | | | | |
|N|O|P|Q|R|S|T|U|V|W|X|Y|Z|

Code Fun - 1

Use the code key at the bottom of this page. Find out what this sentence says. Write the letters on the line.

Code key

A	B	C	D	E	F	G	H	I	J	K	L	M

N	O	P	Q	R	S	T	U	V	W	X	Y	Z

Code Fun - ll

Make your own code. Make a symbol to represent each letter of the alphabet. Draw a symbol under each letter.

A	B	C	D	E	F	G	H	I

J	K	L	M	N	O	P	Q	R

S	T	U	V	W	X	Y	Z

Now write a sentence using your coded symbols. Ask some friends to figure out what your sentence says.

- - - - - - - - - - - - - - - -

- - - - - - - - - - - - - - - -

- - - - - - - - - - - - - - - -

- - - - - - - - - - - - - - - -

Find Your Way

Help the cow find it's way to the green grass!

Explain how you would get from the cow to the green grass using directions: Forward, Back, Left and Right.

Find Your Way

Help the cow find it's way to the green grass!

Explain how you would get from the cow to the green grass using directions:
Up, Down, Left and Right.

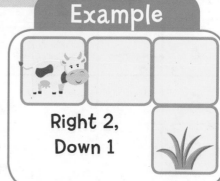
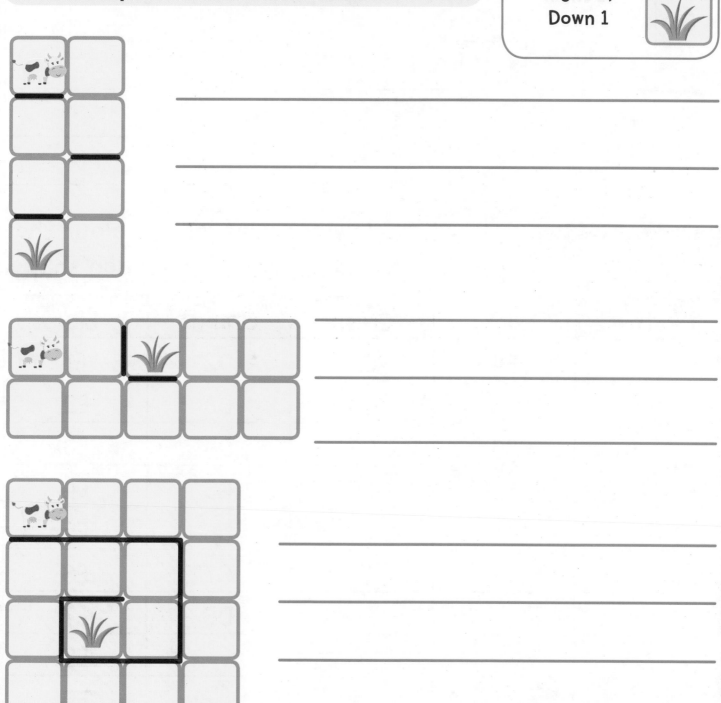

_____

_____

_____

_____

_____

_____

_____

_____

_____

Coding Activity Coordinates Colour In

	1	2	3	4	5	6	7	8	9	10
A										
B										
C										
D										
E										
F										

Instructions Use the below coordinates to colour the above grid and discover the hidden shape.

Purple	Pink	Green	Orange	Blue
A5	B4	C3	D2	E1
	B5	C4	D3	E2
	B6	C5	D4	E3
		C6	D5	E4
		C7	D6	E5
			D7	E6
			D8	E7
				E8
				E9

28

Coding Activity Coordinates Colour In

	1	2	3	4	5	6	7	8	9	10
A										
B										
C										
D										
E										
F										

Instructions Use the below coordinates to colour the above grid and discover the hidden shape.

Green	Pink	Red	Blue
B3	C3	D3	E3
B4	C4	D4	E4
B5	C5	D5	E5
B6	C6	D6	E6
B7	C7	D7	E7
B8	C8	D8	E8

Coding Activity Coordinates Colour In

	1	2	3	4	5	6	7	8	9	10
A										
B										
C										
D										
E										
F										
G										

Instructions Use the below coordinates to colour the above grid and discover the hidden shape.

Red	Blue	Yellow	Purple	Green
A8	B1	A2	A4	A6
B9	B2	A3	B5	A7
C1	C2	B3	B6	B7
D2	C3	B4	C6	B8
E3	C4	C4	C7	C8
F4	D4	C5	D7	C9
G5	E4	D5	D8	
	E5	D6		
	F5	E6		
	F6	E7		

30

Coding Activity Coordinates Colour In

	1	2	3	4	5	6	7	8	9	10	11	12	13	14
A														
B														
C														
D														
E														
F														
G														
H														
I														
J														
K														

Instructions Use the below coordinates to colour the above grid and discover the hidden word.

Red	Blue	Yellow	Green
A2	C5	D10	G12
A3	C6	E10	G13
B1	D4	F8	H11
C1	D7	F9	H14
D1	E4	F10	I11
E2	E7	G7	I12
E3	F4	G10	I13
	G5	H7	I14
	G6	H10	J11
		I8	K12
		I9	K13
		I10	K14

Coding Activity Itsy Bitsy Spider

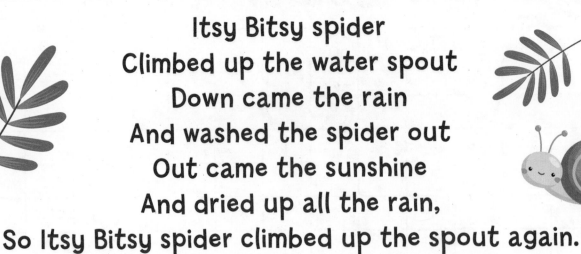

Itsy Bitsy spider
Climbed up the water spout
Down came the rain
And washed the spider out
Out came the sunshine
And dried up all the rain,
So Itsy Bitsy spider climbed up the spout again.

Instructions Draw the arrows and diagrams to create directions to guide someone through the story. Also, write your own instructions down. See Example on the next page.

Itsy Bitsy Spider's Path

Example

Itsy Bitsy Spider

Directions: Forward 2, Turn Right, Forward 2, Turn Left, Forward 3, Turn Right, Forward 1, Turn Right, Forward 5

Coding Activity

Itsy Bitsy Spider
Itsy Bitsy Spider
Climbed up the water spout
Down came the rain.
And washed the spider out.
Out came the sunshine
And dried up all the rain,
So Itsy Bitsy Spider
Climbed up the spout again.

Directions

Use arrows to show the directions required to complete the rhyme in order.
North
East
South
West

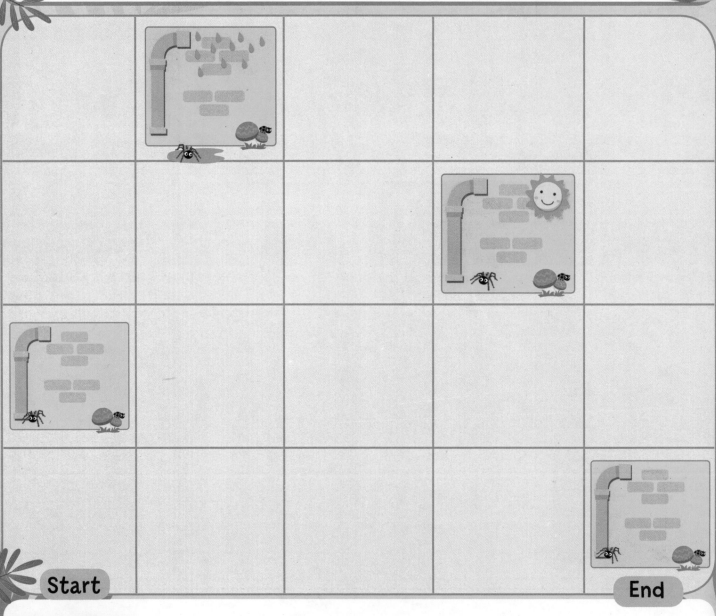

Start

End

Directions

34

Imagine That!

You can change one thing into another just by using your imagination! Imagine a different first letter of each word to get a completely different thing.

middle of your face into a flower

_____ to _____

teddy into fruit

_____ to _____

bird's home into a sleeveless sweater

_____ to _____

finger jewellery into male royalty

_____ to _____

baked dessert into garden tool

_____ to _____

baby bear into bath time place

_____ to _____

Hand in Glove

Some words always seem to go together — like bread and butter! We have collected 11 words pairs for you. Pick a word from a hand and match it to one in a glove. Cross off pairs as you go.

table

pots

stamp

pencil

lock

shoes

socks

pans

chair

fork

pen

key

thread

hide

now

nail

envelope

seek

hammer

knife

then

needle

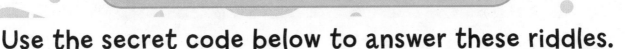

Riddles and Codes

Use the secret code below to answer these riddles.

1. What can run but can't walk?

| 20 | 2 | 12 | 6 | 5 |

2. What can break without being touched?

| 2 | 4 | 5 | 3 | 15 | 16 | 13 | 6 |

3. What is made that can't be seen?

| 9 | 3 | 16 | 13 | 6 |

4. What belongs to you but is used more by others?

| 8 | 3 | 7 | 5 | 9 | 2 | 15 | 6 |

5. What goes up and down without ever moving?

| 13 | 12 | 2 | 16 | 5 | 19 | 2 | 13 | 6 |

6. What is broken when it is spoken?

| 13 | 16 | 17 | 6 | 9 | 19 | 6 |

7. What can be drawn without a pencil?

| 18 | 5 | 6 | 2 | 12 | 11 |

1	2	3	4	5	6	7	8	9	10	11	12	13	14	15	16	17	18	19	20
K	A	O	P	R	E	U	Y	N	F	H	T	S	D	M	I	L	B	C	W

Riddle Time

Solve the clues, write the answer in the boxes provided and when you read down the first column of each group of answers, you will reveal the answer to the riddle. Good luck!

Why couldn't the astronaut land on the moon?

Groom's companion

Number after seven

Art project

Room under the roof

Opposite of over

Begin

Written paper

Bug bites become this

Exchange

Birds have these

Movie participant

Dorsal finned fish

Lost and_____

Saddened

Camel-like animals

Body organ

I have a Special Message

Solve the clues, write the answer in the boxes provided and when you read down the first column of each group of answers, you will find my special message for you.

Group 1 (grid hints: O / T / O / I)
- Accidentally let fall
- Opposite of uncle
- Is this ____book?
- Under garment

Group 2 (grid hints: E / E / E / O / N / R)
- Who's ___ in line?
- Frosted a cake
- Donate ____
- Faith, ____ charity
- Campers dwelling
- Twinkle, twinkle, little ____.

Group 3 (grid hints: O / M / N / O / I / T / E)
- Sweet and ____
- Your house
- Baking chamber
- Lion's sound
- A journey, voyage
- Opposites at enter
- Opposite of front

Group 4 (grid hints: P / V / E / T / A / I)
- Applaud
- Opposite of under
- Opposite of shut
- Opposite of right
- A direction
- ____bow

Group 5 (grid hints: A / R / E / G)
- Musical instrument
- Corn has these?
- One of a kind?
- Chicken by product

Group 6 (grid hints: E / L / E)
- Large primates
- Fasten with
- Loving

Special Message:

_____

39

ANSWERS

Page 4   coding is fun

Page 5   never play with matches

Page 6   answers will vary

Page 7   answers will vary

Page 8      Page 9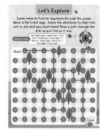

Page 10   answers will vary

Page 11   answers will vary

Page 12      Page 13

Page 14

Page 15   and, be, in, it, of, that, the, to, how

Page 16   has, for, are, with, at, whom, is, on, from

Page 17   coding, memory, screen, disk, copy, cut, save, mouse, paste, print

Page 18   email, internet, virus, keyboard, binary, byte, cable, download, icon, pixel

Page 19   cup, stewpan, vulture, knife, octopus, jellyfish

Page 20   Friday, Tuesday, Sunday, Monday, Wednesday, Saturday, Thursday

Page 21

Page 22   Fee Fie Foe Fum I smell the blood of an Englishman

Page 23   Knowledge is a treasure but practice is the key to it.

Page 24   The old house on the hill is the place that holds all the secrets.

Page 25   answers will vary

Page 26   Forward 4, Forward 1, Turn Right, Forward 2 Down 2, Turn Right Forward, Turn Left Forward 3, Turn Right Forward 3, Turn Left Forward 3, Turn Left Forward 2, Turn Right Forward 2, Turn Right Forward 1, Turn Left.

Page 27   Right 1, Down 1, Left 1 Down 1, Right 1 Down 1, Left 1 Right 1, Down 1, Right 2, Up 1, Left 1 Right 3, Down 3 Left 3, Up 2 Right 2, Down 1 Left 1

Page 28      Page 29

Page 30      Page 31

Page 32   answers will vary

Page 33   answers will vary

Page 34   North 2, East 1

          North 2, East 2

          South 1, East 1

          South 1, West 1

          South 1, East 1

Page 35   Nose to Rose, Bear to Pear, Nest to Vest, Ring to King, Cake to Rake, Cub to Tub

Page 36   table and chair, pen and pencil, fork and knife, thread and needle, now and then, hide and seek, hammer and nail, shoes and socks, pots and pans, envelope and stamp, lock and key

Page 37   Water, A Promise, Noise, Your Name, Staircase, Silence, Breath

Page 38   Bride, Eight, Craft, Attic, Under, Start, Essay, Itchy, Talks   Wings, Actor, Smelt Found, Upset, Llama, Lungs

          Why couldn't the astronaut land on the moon? Because it was full.

Page 39   Drop, Aunt, Your, Slip   Sour, Home, Oven, Roar, Trip, Exit, Rear   Apes, Nail, Dear Next, Iced, Give, Hope, Tent, Star Clap, Over, Open, Left, East, Rain Harp, Ears, Rare, Eggs Special Message: Days shorter and nights cooler here